Tura

This book is on loan from
Library Services for Schools
www.cumbria.gov.uk/libraries/schoolslibserv

County Council

Trailblazers

Formula One
by David Orme
Educational consultant: Helen Bird

Illustrated by Martin Bolchover and Cyber Media (India) Ltd.

Published by Ransom Publishing Ltd.
51 Southgate Street, Winchester, Hants. SO23 9EH
www.ransom.co.uk

ISBN   978 184167 428 5

First published in 2006
Reprinted 2007, 2009

Formula One

Contents

Get the facts   **5**

How did motor racing start?   6

F1 facts   8

Motor racing flags   10

F1 cars   12

A great driver – Michael Schumacher   14

A great British team – McLaren   16

Fiction

The Man of Mystery   19

Formula one word check   **36**

Formula One

Get
the
facts

How did motor racing start?

As soon as cars were invented people wanted to race them.

The first motor race happened in France in 1895.

Cars raced from one town to another and back again.

The race was 1200 kilometres long and it took 48 hours.

The cars travelled at 50 kilometres per hour!

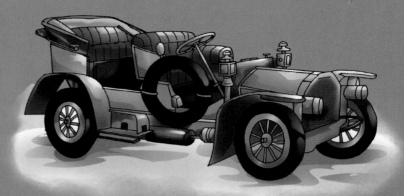

The first Grand Prix race was in 1901. Cars were now going at over 100 kilometres per hour.

By 1930 cars were racing at over 250 kilometres per hour.

Motor racing was very dangerous. There were lots of accidents.

F1 facts

? When was the first formula one motor race?

The first race was in 1950 at Silverstone, in England.

? How long is a formula one race?

About 300 kilometres.

? What does pole position mean?

The car at the front at the start of the race is in pole position. The words pole position come from horse racing.

? How does a car get to be in pole position?

Before the main race the cars see how fast they can go. The fastest car starts at the front.

? Why are the garages called pits?

Years ago, there weren't any garages. The teams dug pits in the ground next to the race track. They could get under the cars to fix them.

? Is motor racing still dangerous?

The cars are very safe, but there are still accidents. In 1994 two racing drivers were killed.

? How fast do formula one cars go?

Cars race at over 300 kilometres per hour.

? Why do formula one cars have wings?

Wings on a plane push it up into the sky. The wings on a formula one car push it down onto the road. This stops it flying off the track.

? Do formula one cars have special tyres?

Yes. After one race they are worn out!

? How many people work for a formula one team?

The McLaren team have over 500 people working for them. The Ferrari team have over 2000!

? What happens in the winter?

Formula one doesn't stop. The teams are busy testing their new cars for the next season.

? Which driver has a number 1 on his car?

The driver who is world champion has the number 1 on his car. No car has a number 13 as drivers think this is an unlucky number.

? How can I become a racing driver?

Many drivers start by racing go-karts. This is a good way to learn the skills you will need to become a formula one driver.

Motor racing flags

What do the flags mean in formula 1?

Yellow flag

Warning. Slow down.
Danger ahead.

Green flag

The track is clear.

Blue Flag

You must let faster
cars overtake you.

Black flag

You have a penalty – go into the pits.

Red and yellow striped flag

Danger! There is oil on the track.

Red Flag

Stop the race NOW.

Chequered flag

The race is over. You have won!

F1 Cars

Driver's cockpit

Drivers need to be slim! They have to take the steering wheel out before getting in or out.

Front wing

The air goes over the top and pushes the car down onto the road.

Brakes

Brakes will only last one race. They glow red hot when they slow the car down.

...ar spoiler

... helps to push the car
...wn onto the road.

Tyres

Tyres are made of soft rubber
to grip the road. They wear
out after one race.

Engine and gearbox

These are made to last
just two races before
they are worn out.

Side pods

Air goes in here to
cool down the engine.

13

A great driver – Michael Schumacher

Michael Schumacher

The world's greatest racing driver!

fact

Michael Schumacher

Born
3rd January 1969 in Germany

Started racing go-karts
1973 (he was four years old!)

First title
European go-kart champion, 1987

First formula one race
1991, for the Jordan team

First World Championship
1994, for the Benetton team

First season with Ferrari   1997

First World Championship win with Ferrari
2000

Best ever season
2002. 11 race wins and 7 pole positions

Number of World Championships by 2005
Seven

box

A great British team – McLaren

History

The McLaren team was started by Bruce McLaren, a racing driver from New Zealand.

The first McLaren car was raced in 1966.

Bruce McLaren was killed testing a car in 1970, but the team carried on.

In 1974 the team won the World Championship for the first time.

The Team is based in Woking, in England.

The great McLaren drivers

Ayrton Senna	Alain Prost	Mika Hakkinen
Drove for McLaren 1988 to 1993	Drove for McLaren 1980, 1984 to 1989	Drove for McLaren 1993 to 2001
World Champion 1988, 1990, 1991	World Champion 1985, 1986, 1989	World Champion 1998, 1999
Killed 1994		

The team Boss – Ron Dennis

Ron Dennis joined McLaren in 1980.

Find out more about McLaren.
Visit their website:
www.mclaren.com

The Man of Mystery

Chapter 1:
The lucky driver

Rick Muggins was the best racing driver in the world. And the luckiest. Everything always seemed to go right for him.

"Guess it's my lucky charm!" Rick said. "I never race without it."

The lucky charm was a locket. It had a picture of a girl inside. It was Rick's girlfriend. She had been killed in a car crash two years ago.

Rick's luck ran out in the last race of the season. There was oil on the track. Cars started to skid, and there was a pile up on a fast corner. Rick's car flipped over. More cars piled up. A car flew up into the air. It landed on Rick. He died on the way to hospital.

When Rick was buried, his lucky charm was around his neck.

Chapter 2:
The man of mystery

At the start of the season a new driver took Rick's place. He was called the Man of Mystery.

He never spoke to reporters, and never took off his helmet. The helmet had specially tinted glass so no-one could see his face. He used the name 'John Smith' but no-one believed that it was his real name.

Everyone wanted to find out who the Man of Mystery really was. But no-one could find him after the race. No-one knew where he lived, or where he went between races.

"He can keep his secrets if he wants," his team boss said. "That's fine by me - as long as he keeps winning races for us!"

Chapter 3:
The best there had ever been

The Man of Mystery was a brilliant driver, even better than Rick had been. His car never let him down. He never got into a skid, even in heavy rain or when there was oil on the track.

No other driver dared to take the risks that 'John Smith' took at every corner.

He wasn't just the best racing driver in the world. He was the best there had ever been. The other drivers were desperate to beat him, but they never had a chance. He always started at the front, and no-one could ever get past him. He won race after race.

Then it was the last race of the season. Could he win this race too?

Chapter 4:
The last race

There were two laps to go. The Man of Mystery was in the lead. But had his luck run out?

There was oil on the road, near the corner where Rick had been killed. A car spun in front of the Man of Mystery. More cars piled in. Cars were flying everywhere.

But out of the wreck roared a battered car. The Man of Mystery was still in the race!

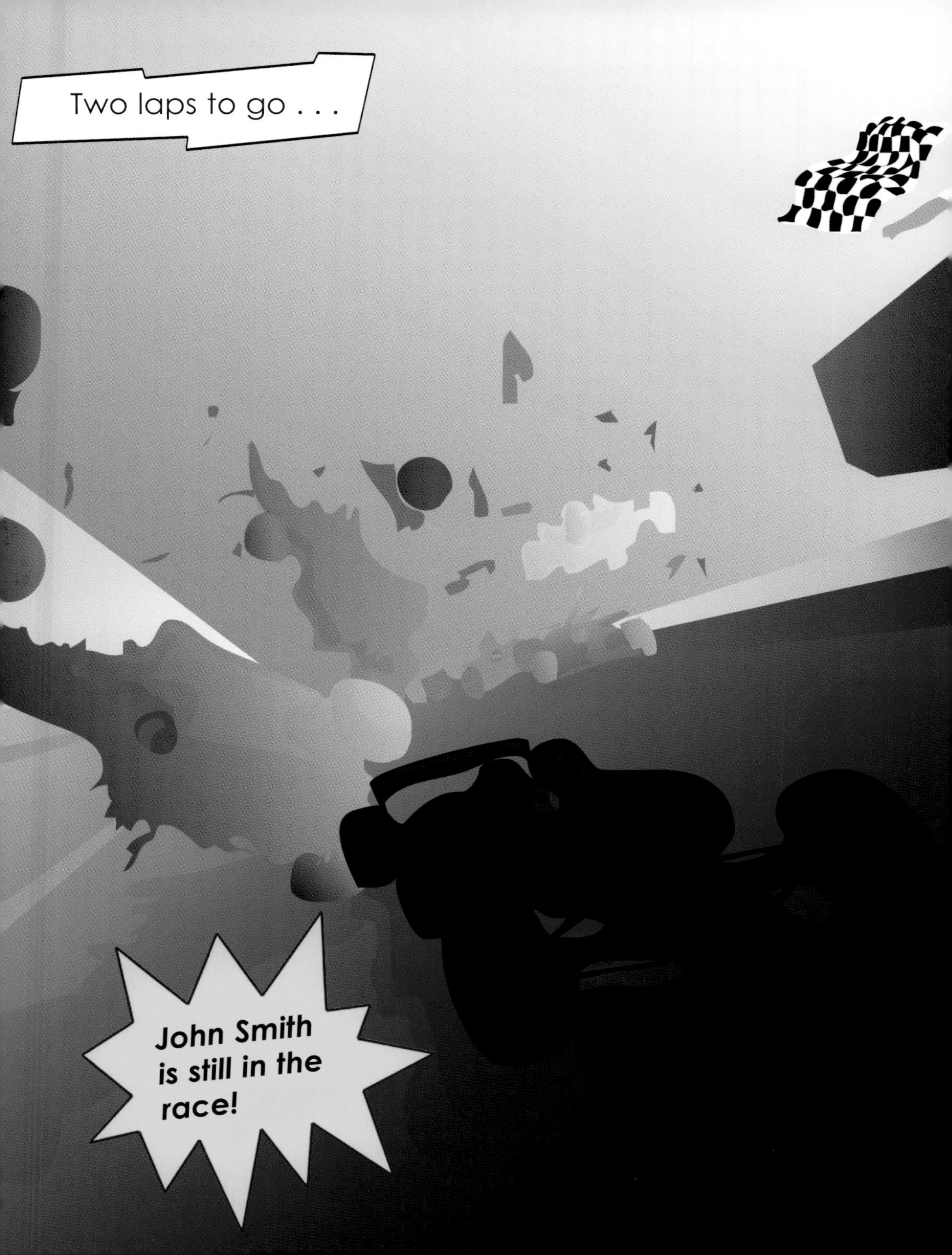
Two laps to go . . .
John Smith is still in the race!

No-one thought he would get to the finish, but he did. The mystery driver had won every race!

But no-one got out of the car. When they looked inside, it was empty. In front of millions, the Man of Mystery had vanished!

But they found something on the car seat. It was Rick Muggins' locket.

Inside was the picture of Rick's girlfriend. And next to her in the picture, was Rick himself.

Formula one word check

accidents

battered

believed

brilliant

buried

chequered flag

cockpit

danger

dangerous

desperate

engine

England

flipped

formula one

garages

gearbox

girl friend

Grand Prix

heavy

hospital

invented

kilometres

laps

locket

lucky charm

millions

mystery

New Zealand

overtake

penalty

pole position

reporters

season

skid

slim

special

spoiler

steering wheel

tyres

unlucky

vanished

warning

World Championship